5 STEPS TO *Making Disciples*

STUDY GUIDE

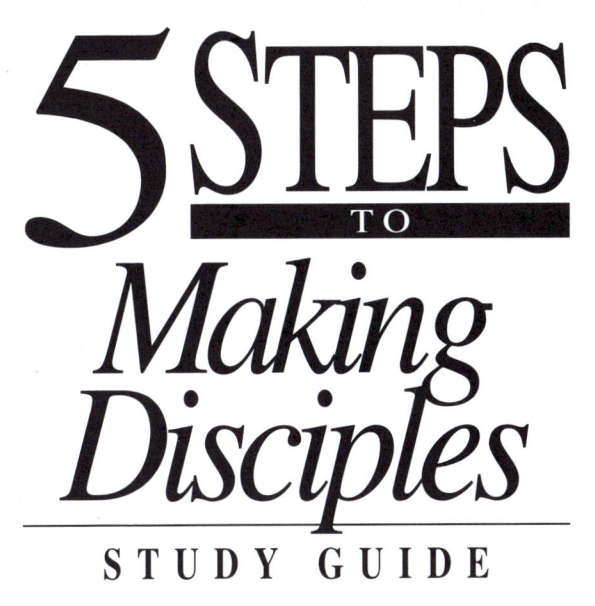

Bill Bright

NewLife
PUBLICATIONS
A MINISTRY OF CAMPUS CRUSADE FOR CHRIST

Five Steps to Making Disciples
Study Guide

Published by
NewLife Publications
A ministry of Campus Crusade for Christ
P.O. Box 593684
Orlando, FL 32859-3684

© 1997, Bill Bright. All rights reserved. No part of this publication may be reproduced, stored in a retrieval system, or transmitted in any form or by any means, except in the case of brief quotations printed in articles or reviews, without prior permission in writing from the publisher.

Design and typesetting by Genesis Publications.

Printed in the United States of America.

Distributed in Canada by Campus Crusade for Christ of Canada, Surrey, B.C.

ISBN 1-56399-056-3

NewLife2000 is a registered service mark of Campus Crusade for Christ Inc.

Unless otherwise indicated, all Scripture references are taken from the *New International Version*, © 1973, 1978, 1984 by the International Bible Society. Published by Zondervan Bible Publishers, Grand Rapids, Michigan.

As a personal policy, Bill Bright has never accepted honorariums or royalties for his personal use. Any royalties from this book or the more than fifty books and booklets by Bill Bright are dedicated to the glory of God and designated to the various ministries of Campus Crusade for Christ/*NewLife2000*.

For more information, write:
Life Ministries—P.O. Box 40, Flemington Markets, N5W 2129, Australia
Campus Crusade for Christ of Canada—Box 300, Vancouver, B.C., V6C 2X3, Canada
Campus Crusade for Christ—Fairgate House, King's Road, Tyseley, Birmingham, B11 2AA, England
Campus Crusade for Christ—P.O. Box 8786, Auckland, New Zealand
Campus Crusade for Christ—Alexandra, P.O. Box 0205, Singapore, 9115, Singapore
Great Commission Movement of Nigeria—P.O. Box 500, Jos, Plateau State Nigeria, West Africa
Campus Crusade for Christ International—100 Sunport Lane, Orlando, FL 32809, USA

Contents

A Personal Word 5
The Principle of Spiritual Multiplication .7
Steps:
- **1** Answer God's Call to Discipleship 11
- **2** Begin a Discipleship Ministry .17
- **3** Establish Personal Relationships 21
- **4** Inspire Others to Grow in Their Faith 27
- **5** Prepare to Lead a Discipleship Group 35

Resources to Help You Make Disciples 43

A Personal Word

Of all the great challenges you have heard of or participated in, which one brings the most joy and benefit? I have found that nothing compares with the privilege of introducing others to Christ, thereby helping to fulfill the Great Commission as given by our Lord in Matthew 20:18–20. That is my firm conviction, and my experience over the years has confirmed it.

Someone once asked, "In light of your long ministry for our Lord and the lessons you have learned since you started Campus Crusade for Christ in 1951, what would you do differently?"

This was a topic about which I had strong convictions, so I responded, "I would concentrate more on winning and training men and women of God (building disciples) whom He has already chosen and ordained to be His spokesmen to the world."

That is what Jesus emphasized in the Great Commission and what the apostle Paul instructed Timothy, his son in the faith, as recorded in 2 Timothy 2:2:

> The things you have heard me say in the presence of many witnesses entrust to reliable men who will also be qualified to teach others.

Although Campus Crusade's major thrust since its inception has been winning others to Christ, building them in their faith, training and discipling believers to become fruitful witnesses, then sending them out to help fulfill the Great Commission, my conviction about its importance has intensified. If I could change my past ministry, I would place a greater emphasis on building disciples who are committed to the fulfillment of the Great Commission. For those who respond to the call, I would seek to inspire, motivate, and train them to understand the greatness of God and His plan for men and women.

There is no question in my mind that the prayers and witness of godly, Spirit-filled men and women can reverse the tide of evil that is threatening to destroy all that we hold dear and sacred in our Judeo-Christian faith. The key to changing the world is spiritual multiplication—winning and training men and women who in turn win and train others who go on to win and train still others, spiritual generation after spiritual generation. (This principle is explained more fully in the next section.) That is the strategy the church used in the first centuries to reach the world with God's message. And it is the same strategy we are using to touch the lives of people all over the world today.

This principle is seen so clearly in the life of a Thai Christian whom I met some time ago. Charlie Wanagit was at that time the spiritual father of twelve generations of believers. Charlie, who had led more than 1,500 people to Christ in the past four years, introduced me to one of his disciples, who introduced me to one of his disciples, and so it went down a line of twelve men and women. The last disciple in the chain had been a Christian only six months and had already introduced twelve people to Christ!

But tragically, many Christians today are not true disciples of our Lord Jesus Christ. Instead, they are content to "play church" while living a materialistic and selfish lifestyle. Yet many others have demonstrated sacrificial love for God and for building His kingdom.

God is an all-powerful, loving, wise, and compassionate heavenly Father! Nothing is too hard for Him. He is looking for true disciples—men and women who are willing to put their lives on the line for Him, who will use their resources to win, build, train, and send others in order to help fulfill the Great Commission. I challenge you to be part of His plan to take the most joyful news ever announced of His love and forgiveness to every person on earth. God will richly bless you for your obedience, and you will experience the reality of our Lord's promise to reveal Himself to all who love and obey Him (John 14:21).

> Only one life, 'twill soon be past;
> only what's done for Christ will last.

The Principle of Spiritual Multiplication

Imagine for a moment that you are a great evangelist. The intense desire of your heart is to help fulfill the Great Commission (Matthew 28:18–20) that Christ gave us before He left this earth. You share the message of God's love and forgiveness through Jesus Christ wherever you go and 1,000 people each day come to Christ as a result of your ministry.

At that rate, how long do you think it would take you to reach the world for Christ? Assuming that the population did not grow, it would take approximately 15,000 years!

This is what I call spiritual addition. But God has given His children a miraculous strategy called spiritual multiplication through which we can reach the world in our generation. Spiritual multiplication is purposefully discipling new Christians so that they in turn will evangelize and disciple others, spiritual generation after spiritual generation.

Boonma Panthrasi, our director in Thailand, is an amazing example of spiritual multiplication. He and his wife, Chalong, received their training at our Great Commission Training Center in the Philippines in 1980. They returned to Thailand, and within six years he trained 700 individuals to share their faith in Christ and teach others to do the same. In turn, these disciples have trained 90,000 and are now involved in winning and discipling still others.

For example, Boonma trained Boonhiang, a new Christian, how to follow-up new believers. Boonhiang was so excited about his Lord that he would not go one day without talking to others about Jesus Christ. Soon, he became part of a "JESUS" film team, traveling with the group to show the "JESUS" film all over the area. Since he used the *Four Spiritual Laws* as a witnessing tool, he asked Boonma to make a flip chart with the words and diagrams so he could use it to speak to large groups. As soon as he received the flip chart, he carried it wherever he went.

As of today, Boonhiang has personally shared his faith in Christ with 200,000 people. And more than 20,000 have received Christ through this man's witness. At 74 years of age, Boonhiang is still active for his Lord and can count more than forty spiritual generations of Christians involved in evangelism and discipleship. As a result, the church he leads in his hometown has fourteen daughter churches. His witness is so vibrant that he receives many invitations to pioneer a work in another area or to debate with native religious radicals, including many Buddhists. In the long run, he wins his arguments, but does so with peace. He has introduced many of his listeners to Jesus Christ.

But Boonhiang's zeal for the Lord has also come with a price. He has suffered persecution for his faith, but God has always protected him. He has been stoned. He has been shot at by gangsters—but all their bullets missed. Thieves who tried to rob him were blinded. When Communists trapped him in the jungle, he boldly witnessed to them. Some of them received Christ, and after four days he was released unharmed. His example emphasizes the importance of training new believers how to witness effectively and boldly for our Lord and to persevere in following Him.

These believers know that it is not enough just to lead others to the Lord, and say, "Isn't it great?"—then leave them alone to grow spiritually by themselves. Rather, these spiritual multipliers win people and disciple them, training the new Christians to win and disciple others so they, in turn, will win and disciple still others. If we properly communicate the basic principles of our faith to new Christians, many will grow into spiritual multipliers.

I am often reminded of the personal motto of my beloved friend, Dawson Trotman, founder of the Navigators: "Born to reproduce." That describes New Testament Christianity. Boonhiang's ministry is a dramatic example of that concept of New Testament Christianity in our century.

You and I can be spiritual multipliers, too. If each of us would win just one person to Christ and train him to disciple others, who would in turn win and disciple others, we could reach the world for Christ in this generation!

I encourage you before this day is over to ask yourself, "Am I committed to influencing my world for Jesus Christ? If so, am I giving myself to spiritual multiplication or to spiritual addition?" If you have a desire to build spiritual qualities into the lives of others, ask God to lead you to several individuals through whom you can build a chain of multipliers. Then give to these brothers and sisters in Christ your vision for the Great Commission and the importance of spiritual multiplication. Watch how God will use you to reach people you could never touch through spiritual addition.

The lessons in this book were designed to help you teach other Christians how to reproduce spiritually. By the end of these five Steps, your students will be ready to begin their own multiplying ministries. As you lead your small group study, you will see your members get excited about leading their own group and showing individuals whom they have introduced to Christ how to do the same. In time, your group can multiply into many groups which will in turn produce even more groups. By studying and leading these five lessons, you will learn how to:

- Follow-up new and older Christians
- Motivate and encourage others to make disciples
- Help group members lead their own discipleship groups

Enjoy the excitement of seeing your disciples become disciplers, resulting in a dynamic ministry right in your community! I am confident that our Lord will multiply your ministry as you begin to train others.

STEP 1

Answer God's Call to Discipleship

The Discipleship Ministry of Jesus

Discuss the principles with your group and write down the most pertinent points.

1. Jesus prayed for His disciples (John 17:9–11).

   Jesus pray to God to protect his peoples knowing the God had all

2. Jesus taught them God's Word (Luke 24:44–48).

3. Jesus depended on God and the power of the Holy Spirit (John 5:30; Luke 4:1).

4. Jesus trained His disciples and sent them out to minister (Matthew 28:18–20; Mark 3:13,14; Acts 1:8).

5. Jesus urged His disciples to take steps of faith (Matthew 14:22–32).

6. Jesus emphasized an eternal perspective (Matthew 6:19–21).

7. Jesus initiated and modeled evangelism (Luke 8:1; John 4:27–42).

8. Jesus was an example of servanthood (Matthew 20:28; John 13:1–17).

Questions for Reflection
- What is most significant to you about Jesus' discipleship ministry?

- How did Jesus use both words and actions in training others?

- How have you seen this combination work in your ministry?

Example of a Disciple-Maker

The following passages show characteristics in Paul's life that made him a good disciple-maker. Write the qualities after each reference. How is each quality displayed in your life?

STEP 1

- Romans 8:9; 2 Corinthians 2:4

- 1 Corinthians 9:24–27

- Philippians 1:20,21

- Philippians 3:8

- Colossians 1:24–29

- 2 Timothy 4:17,18

- Hebrews 13:17

Our Responsibility

How do these points fit in with 1 Corinthians 3:5–9 and our responsibility in disciple-making?

1. We are God's instruments on earth.

2. We have the privilege and responsibility to nurture new Christians and create an environment that encourages spiritual growth.

Not everyone we introduce to Christ or challenge to begin a discipleship ministry will follow through with a commitment to making disciples. Remember, ultimately, God is responsible for spiritual growth. We cannot make anyone mature in their faith. Our responsibility is to follow Christ's commands and His example for discipleship and leave the results to God.

The Call to Make Disciples

Jesus calls us to make disciples of others. Matthew 28:18–20 and Colossians 1:28,29 are parallel in five main points about the call to make disciples. Read each item, then consider this question: What impact does the point have on my ministry? Write your conclusions here:

- The authority and power are from Jesus.

- The imperative is to disciple others.

- The scope is the whole world.

- The task is both evangelism and discipleship.

STEP 1

- The expectation is that Jesus will bless us in our work.

Look up each set of verses and discuss how these characteristics help us in a discipleship ministry. Answer this question for each point: Given this information, what is God asking you to do differently?

- Love others (John 13:34,35; Philippians 2:4).

- Obediently apply His Word to our lives (John 14:23,24; 1 John 5:3).

- Fish for men (Matthew 4:19).

- Pray according to God's will (1 John 5:14,15).

- Depend moment by moment on the power of the Holy Spirit (Acts 1:8; Ephesians 5:18).

- Suffer with and for Jesus (Philippians 1:29,30).

Answering the Call to Discipleship

Action Point: After studying the biblical call to make disciples, how committed are you to making disciples? Silently review these questions as you consider your ministry. Write down ways you will implement changes.

1. Am I presently depending on Jesus' power in my life and ministry? How can I deepen this dependence?

2. Do I view making disciples as an imperative in my life and ministry? How can I increase my vision and concern?

3. Does my personal ministry have "reaching the world" as its objective? How can I broaden my ministry?

4. Is my evangelism resulting in faithful disciples and are my faithful disciples being trained in evangelism?

    In what ways can I allow the Lord to work more fully in me toward these goals?

5. Am I working hard in the power of the Holy Spirit and am I expecting Jesus to bless the work?

    How can I allow the Holy Spirit to become more effective as He works through me?

STEP 2

Begin a Discipleship Ministry

The Elements of Spiritual Multiplication

Read 2 Timothy 2:1–10. Note the elements of spiritual multiplication found in verses 1 and 2.

1. The power for spiritual multiplication (verse 1)

2. The pattern for spiritual multiplication (verse 2)

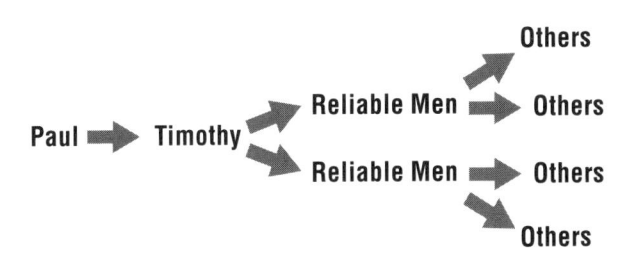

```
                              → Others
               → Reliable Men → Others
Paul → Timothy
               → Reliable Men → Others
                              → Others
```

- What promises does Jesus give in Matthew 28:18–20?

- Why are the promises so significant?

- Since it is God's will for you to make disciples, how does the promise in Philippians 2:13 relate to this command?

The Motivation for Spiritual Multiplication

1.

2.

3.

Our motivation to disciple:

Why do we serve as disciplers? Fill in the following points:

1. Romans 3:10–18

2. John 9:4

3. Matthew 28:19; Acts 1:8

STEP 2   19

Our Potential Impact

This diagram gives you an idea of what one person can do.

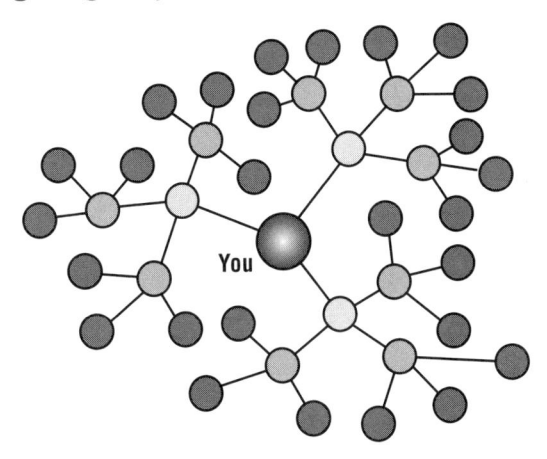

The following chart gives an effective method for multiplying spiritually.

Process for Building Multiplying Disciples				
	Part 1	**Part 2**	**Part 3**	**Part 4**
PRINCIPLE	Win	Build	Train	Send
METHOD	Present the gospel, evangelism	Follow-up appointments and Christian growth Bible study: new Christians learn assurance of salvation and walking in power of Holy Spirit	Discipleship groups: members learn to witness	Multiplication groups: members start their own groups

	Process for Building Multiplying Disciples *(continued)*			
	Part 1	**Part 2**	**Part 3**	**Part 4**
MATERIALS	*Four Spiritual Laws*, *"JESUS"* video, *A Man Without Equal* video and book, *Jesus and the Intellectual* or *A Great Adventure* booklets	*Five Steps of Christian Growth* Bible study	*Five Steps to Sharing Your Faith* Bible study or *Reaching Your World* video series	*Five Steps to Making Disciples* Bible study
TRAINING LEVEL	Basic training	Intermediate training	Advanced training	Leadership training

Action Point: The areas in my community that the Lord is laying on my heart to influence for Christ are:

As a result of studying spiritual multiplication in God's Word, I want to take the following steps:

1. *Witness:* As an act of faith, I will commit this week to share my faith in Christ with an unbelieving friend.

    Name: _____

2. *Discipleship group:* To begin my ministry of discipleship, I will begin asking God to bring people whom I can disciple into a discipleship group. I will begin praying for the people I list here:

    _____
    _____
    _____
    _____

STEP 3

Establish Personal Relationships

Basics of Follow-Up

Definition: Follow-up is the process by which new believers are established in the faith and equipped with the basics of Christianity so they can grow toward spiritual maturity and become multiplying disciples.

What part does each of the following principles play in the follow-up process?

1. Remember that God causes the spiritual growth (1 Corinthians 3:6,7; Philippians 1:6; 2:13).

2. Build relationships with new believers (Acts 2:41,42,46).

3. Motivate new believers to grow spiritually (2 Peter 3:18).

4. Introduce new believers to God's desire for all Christians to witness (Acts 1:8).

5. Encourage new Christians to become involved with other believers (Hebrews 10:24,25).

6. Pray regularly for those you follow-up (Colossians 4:12).

7. Meet regularly with new believers and teach them how to live Spirit-filled lives (Acts 11:25,26; Ephesians 5:18).

8. Challenge new believers and more mature Christians to become multiplying disciples (2 Timothy 2:2).

Purpose of follow-up: Christ sends us out to introduce others to Him, to help them become His disciples, and to teach them how to reach out to others (Matthew 28:18–20).

Paul's Example of Follow-Up

Write the four main points from Paul's example of follow-up, then answer the questions.

1.

How can you identify with those in your ministry?

2.

STEP 3

Why is it important to teach "all of God's Word?" What does this mean?

3.

What values and responsibilities do you want to teach new believers? Why are these important to know?

4.

What will it cost you to become a disciple-maker?

Making a Follow-Up Appointment

How to Make a Follow-Up Appointment

1. Seek an appointment to meet with new believers within 24 to 48 hours. It is important to meet with new Christians right away since they are so vulnerable to Satan's attacks.
2. Arrange a specific time and place convenient for both of you.
3. Encourage the new Christian to review the *Four Spiritual Laws* before you meet again. Then pray together, thanking the Lord Jesus once more for coming into your lives. Also encourage the person to read the first three chapters of John before the appointment. (If he does not have a Bible, offer to give him one.)

Use the Dialog Example on the next page to practice making a follow-up appointment. Adapt it to your situation.

Action Point: Write the name of two or more new Christians or mature believers you will ask to set up an appointment. Then pray for your contact with each person. Before the next session, make a follow-up appointment with each person, but schedule these appointments after the next session because the lesson will cover how to conduct a follow-up appointment.

_____

_____

_____

STEP 3

Dialog Example

Terry: Jack, when you invited Christ into your life today, you began a personal relationship with Him. But this is really only the beginning. You and I just met. In this sense we have begun a friendship, a personal relationship, too. But what if, after today, we never see or hear from each other again. Will our friendship grow?

Jack: No.

Terry: Why not?

Jack: Because a friendship depends on getting to know each other.

Terry: Right, and it's the same way with our Lord Jesus Christ. Even though you began a relationship with Him today, for you to grow, you need to know Him better. The better we know God, the more we can trust and obey Him. How do you think a friendship grows?

Jack: By spending time together, talking to each other and doing things together.

Terry: That's right. And we need to learn how to communicate with Christ and allow Him to communicate with us. That's why we spend time with Him. I'd like to get together with you again and share how you can build your friendship with God. Would you be interested?

Jack: Yes, I would.

Terry: Are you free next week at this time?

Jack: Yes.

Terry: Why don't we meet right here? Let's write that down.

Jack: Okay, that will be fine.

Terry: I encourage you to read through the *Four Spiritual Laws* again before we meet and thank Christ that He is in your life. By thanking God you demonstrate faith, and that pleases Him. You may also want to read the first three chapters of the Gospel of John before we meet.

I really enjoyed talking with you. I look forward to seeing you this time next week.

STEP 4

Inspire Others to Grow in Their Faith

Guidelines for Follow-Up

How do you think each of these guidelines contributes to the follow-up appointment?

1. *Have a clear objective for each appointment.* Keeping the objective in mind will help you stay on the subject.

2. *Establish rapport with the new Christian.* It is important to establish rapport during the first few minutes of the appointment. Be enthusiastic, be friendly, and seek to create in the new believer a desire to grow in Christ. Ask how things have gone since you last met.

3. *Ask if he has read the material you gave him at your last meeting.* Help him with any questions he might have.

4. *Go through the follow-up material.* For example, during the first appointment, review the *Four Spiritual Laws*.

5. *Be relaxed but attentive to the person's needs.* Watch the time, and if the person has other obligations to keep, cut the time short. On the other hand, do not hurry away if the new believer wants to talk about personal issues. He may be more open to talking now than he was before.

Follow these guidelines when closing your appointment:

- *Let him know that you enjoyed your time together,* and that you would like to meet again to talk more about God and the Christian life.

- *Encourage him to join your Bible study group.* Tell him the time and place, and offer to give him a ride if he feels hesitant. Personal follow-up is a bridge to group follow-up. It is important to involve new believers with other Christians as soon as possible, because without the support of other Christians, few new believers grow to spiritual maturity.

- *Invite him to attend church* with you or recommend a Christ-honoring church in his area.

- *Invite him to go witnessing with you.* Witnessing is an important tool for discipleship, and new believers should be encouraged to participate as soon as they are ready.

- *Close your appointment in prayer.*

Conducting a Follow-Up Appointment

Record the procedures for using the *Four Spiritual Laws* follow-up material:

1.

2.

STEP 4

3.

4.

Observing the procedures used in conducting a follow-up appointment will be very helpful to you as you prepare for your own appointments. Write your observations of the class demonstration here:

Evaluation: Evaluating your personal rehearsal is valuable to you. Write your observations of your practice session here:

What improvements would you like to make in your presentation?

Action Point: Apply what you have learned in these lessons with the people you are currently following up. Record how you plan to use this information in your personal ministry:

Use the space below to list those you contact for follow-up appointments and to describe the results. Keep track of times and dates and how the appointments went. Remember: your goal is to get new believers involved in a Bible study group.

Sample Conversation for the First Follow-Up Appointment

The following Sample Conversation should be used as a guideline for conducting a follow-up appointment. Do not use it word for word. Instead, communicate the content in a natural way. Remember, the Lord is concerned with people, not methods. His Holy Spirit does the work through us—the methods just help us to be more efficient.

Terry: Jack, I'm glad we're able to get together again. Have you thought any more about our discussion yesterday?

Jack: Yes, I have. But I'm still trying to understand what all this will mean in my life.

Terry: I can identify with that. As I mentioned yesterday, when you invited Christ into your life, you began a new relationship. It takes time to get to know Him. I had the same thoughts you have and that's why I'm excited about getting together with you and explaining some of these things to you. I had a friend who did that with me and it really helped. Did you have a chance to review the *Four Spiritual Laws* and thank God for coming into your life?

Jack: Yes, but I fell asleep before I could read any of the Gospel of John.

Terry: I understand. I sometimes have trouble staying awake at night too. I want to encourage you to begin reading through that Gospel. It will give you a clear picture of who Christ is. Do you have any questions about the things we talked about yesterday?

Jack: Not right now.

Terry: Okay, then let's review the part in the *Four Spiritual Laws* on how we can know Christ is in our life. Let's look at the questions together.

[Turn to page 11 in your *Four Spiritual Laws* booklet.]

Terry: I'll read the questions and look up the verse in my Bible. Then we'll discuss them.

STEP 4

Jack: That sounds good.

Terry: The first questions is: Did you receive Christ into your life?

Jack: Yes.

Terry: According to His promise in Revelation 3:20, where is Jesus Christ right now in relation to you?

Jack: In my heart.

Terry: That's right. Christ said that he would come into your life. Would He mislead you?

Jack: No.

Terry: On what authority do you know that God has answered your prayer when you invited Christ into your life?

Jack: He said He would come in.

Terry: That's right. Our faith is in the trustworthiness of God and His Word.

[Finish the rest of the booklet in the same manner.]

Terry: Well, Jack, I enjoyed going through this booklet with you. I hope it was helpful.

Jack: Yes, it really was. I didn't realize God gave us so many promises in the Bible.

Terry: Right after I received Christ, it helped to have my friend show me additional truths about God and answer my questions. I am going to join [or lead] a Bible study group that will help Christians grow spiritually. Are you interested in participating in a group like that?

Jack: Yes, but what would be involved?

Terry: The Bible study group will meet once a week for an hour. In this group, you can bring up any questions you might have about your new life in Christ and you will get to know other Christians.

Jack: That sounds really interesting to me.

Terry: Great. It begins on Tuesday at 8 o'clock. Is that good for you?

Jack: Yes, that would be fine.

Terry: I'll call you on Monday to remind you. Would you like me to pick you up?

Jack: That's a good idea.

Terry: I am so excited about what God is doing. In fact, I really enjoy talking with others about my faith in Christ. Would you like to go with me as I explain to someone else about Christ like I did with you yesterday?

Jack: Well, I'm not sure I'm ready for that. Would I have to say anything?

Terry: No. you can just listen. I'd really enjoy the company. Would Saturday afternoon be good for you?

Jack: Sure, I could make that.

Terry: Good. I'll come by and pick you up around 1:30.

Jack: Thanks. I'll be waiting. See you then.

[In the next few weeks, invite the new Christian to attend church with you and spend time together in a social setting. For instance, you could invite him to join you for lunch after church.]

Outline for the Second Follow-Up Appointment

Objective: To help the new believer understand and practice Spirit-filled living.

1. Read Romans 8:35–39. Discuss how permanent God's love is.

2. Read John 10:10. Discuss how God wants us to have an exciting, abundant life. Ask, "Why do many Christians fail to experience this abundant life?" *(Because they do not surrender every part of their life to God or have unconfessed sin in their life.)*

3. Read Romans 8:5–8. Explain how unconfessed sin short-circuits the flow of God's power. Say, "Confessing sin immediately keeps your relationship with God vital and growing."

4. Ask, "If Christ has already paid the penalty for our sins, why should we confess them?" *(Christ has forgiven us once and for all. By confessing our sins, we show that we agree that our action is wrong in God's eyes and that we understand what God has done for us through Jesus.)*

5. Ask, "Does God stop loving us when we sin?" *(No.)*

6. Say, "We can stop being worldly and sinful and experience God's love and forgiveness by practicing Spiritual Breathing. Describe the process of physical breathing: we breathe in pure air and exhale impure air. Compare what happens to your body if you stop breathing with what happens to your spiritual life if you do not confess sin. Emphasize that you cannot lose your spiritual life, but you can become useless to God if you are bound in sin.

7. Read 1 John 1:9 and explain exhaling—confessing our sin.

8. Read Ephesians 5:18 and explain inhaling—appropriating the power of the Holy Spirit as an act of our will by faith.

9. Lead the new believer in Spiritual Breathing:

    Exhale:

    Ask the Holy Spirit to bring to your mind any unconfessed sin.

    Confess your sin and claim the promise of 1 John 1:9.

    Make restitution for the sin if necessary.

    Inhale:

    Claim the filling of the Spirit by faith as commanded in Ephesians 5:18 and promised in 1 John 5:14,15.

10. Encourage the new believer to start a habit of daily Bible reading. Read aloud Psalm 119:97–100 and 1 Peter 2:2. Explain how God's Word is food for our new life in Christ. Encourage him to begin by reading one chapter of the New Testament each day, beginning with the Gospel of John.

11. Emphasize that memorizing Scripture is an excellent way to make God's Word a part of his life. Write John 3:16; 1 John 1:9; Matthew 28:18–20; Ephesians 2:8,9; and Romans 8:1,2 on a slip of paper or a card. Give it to him and ask him to memorize one verse each day, reviewing each he has learned every day.

12. Explain to the new believer how to have a quiet time with God.

13. Encourage the new believer again to learn more about his new life in Christ by joining a Bible study group.

14. If the new believer is still hesitant about joining a Bible study group or your group is not yet meeting, arrange to meet again. Together, go over 2 Timothy 3:16,17; Philippians 4:6,7; Hebrews 10:24,25; and John 14:21.

15. Pray together, thanking God for His love and forgiveness.

[Encourage your disciple to read the Transferable Concept, *How to Love by Faith*. Obtain the booklet at a Christian bookseller or call New*Life* Publications at (800) 235-7255 to order.]

STEP 5

Prepare to Lead a Discipleship Group

Your Leadership Role

Following are the principles of good leadership:

1. *A good leader builds an atmosphere of trusting God* (John 14:1). Our Lord must be the focus of our study groups. We do not merely study about God, we get to know Him personally and learn to trust Him with every area of our life and ministry.

2. *A good leader encourages a mindset of ministering to others* (Romans 15:2; 1 John 3:17). We do not want to become ingrown (considering only our own interests), but rather reach out to others to meet their needs.

3. *A good leader cultivates an attitude of loving relationships* (John 13:34). Many factors can cause people to join a group, but only loving, Christ-centered relationships will keep them involved.

4. *A good leader creates a vision for reaching his community and the world* (Matthew 24:14). Acquiring a vision does not happen by itself; the leader must help the vision develop. Help students find a vision for helping to fulfill the Great Commission by praying together for your community and the world and by sharing witnessing experiences.

5. *A good leader provides loving accountability for group members* (Galatians 6:1,2). Greater spiritual growth results when Christians encourage each other to do the right thing. Here are ways you can help group members be accountable:

a. *Get involved in their lives.* Do not just meet once a week, but get involved in the day-to-day lives of others and encourage them to do the same.

b. *Help members apply God's holy Word to their lives.* Study the Bible with them, then model how to live the principles. Help them apply what they are learning to specific areas of their lives. Encourage them to set spiritual goals and pray with them about achieving these goals.

c. *Minister together.* Practical application is essential to learning. Imagine a doctor learning how to do surgery from a book! To help members, walk alongside them as they develop the necessary skills to witness, conduct follow-up appointments, and lead a group. Then hold them accountable for using their skills.

Leadership Questionnaire

Jot down a skeleton of your normal weekly schedule:

Sunday:

Monday:

Tuesday:

Wednesday:

Thursday:

Friday:

Saturday:

---

1. What activities can I eliminate as time wasters?

2. What blocks of time can I best use for ministry?

3. What blocks of time will I mark off for other responsibilities, such as family time, personal needs, or fun?

4. How can I change my discipleship ministry to help maximize my time for the Lord?

Step 5

The Role of a Discipleship Group

A Plan to Evangelize
My plan for evangelism is:

An Environment for Growth
We must help our disciples become active members of the body of Christ, not just a part of our ministry group.

Read Romans 12:3–8 and 1 Corinthians 3:5–9 and answer these questions.

- What might happen if students are limited to one person's leadership for an extended period of time?

- What are some ways we are connected to other ministries?

- How can being a part of a church and of other ministries contribute to members' growth?

Discipleship is an exciting ministry for many reasons. Lively interaction with a variety of people and growing interpersonal relationships provide an enriching experience. These are the main elements of a healthy group environment.

1. *Sharing:* In your opinion, why is a sharing time important for connecting with each other?

2. *Prayer and praise time:* How has prayer helped you during our study times?

3. *Discussion:* In your opinion, what are the pitfalls of a discussion time? How can a leader help eliminate them?

4. *Building a vision:* How has your vision changed as a result of attending this group?

5. *Training:* How has this training helped you in your witnessing?

6. *One-on-one help:* What might happen to individual spiritual growth without one-on-one training outside of class time?

7. *Personal relationships:* What has been the most enjoyable for you during the weeks our group has met?

Selecting Disciples

It is important to look for the following qualities in the Christians we disciple. The person who is growing in these areas will likely become a good disciple-maker. For each person you plan to ask to join your new discipleship group, use the following list to evaluate his qualities as a potential disciple.

Qualities of a Potential Disciple

1. *A heart for God:* Does the person have a deep commitment to seek God? Here are some ways to tell:

   What does he talk about?

   Does his conversation tend to center around the Lord?

   Do his decisions glorify God?

2. *Dependence on the Holy Spirit:* Does the person demonstrate the fruit of the Spirit (Galatians 5:22,23) in daily life?

   Does he demonstrate faith in tough circumstances?

   How does he respond when things do not go well?

3. *Teachability:* Does this person ask questions about God's Word and ministry?

4. *Ability to build relationships:* Does the person have close friends?

   Do people like to be around him?

   Does he like to be around people?

   Does he give of himself to others?

5. *Relational thinking* (relating all areas of life to an ultimate purpose of glorifying God): Does this person have the purpose in life to glorify God?

   Does he relate decisions to this purpose and organize life's details around this purpose?

6. *Availability:* God is not looking for people with exceptional ability, but those who will be available for His work. Will this person make time for witnessing and being part of a Bible study? Does he follow through with his commitments or does he begin a task to abandon it when something more "exciting" comes along?

Steps to selecting disciples:

1. Ask God if He is leading you to work with this person.
2. Meet with this person individually and share your vision for fulfilling the biblical call to spiritual multiplication. Be specific about how God can use a small group in these ways:
   - To help him in his spiritual growth and ministry
   - To contribute to his fellowship and relationships
   - To provide personal training in how to share his faith
3. Explain what is required of a member in your discipleship group: to model godly living in your Christian life, a commitment of time, and witnessing as a lifestyle.
4. Give him a few days to think over his decision. Tell him that you will be praying for him, and that you will check with him on a certain date to find out his answer. Assure him that a "no" answer will not change your relationship.

Leading the First Meeting

The following practical tips will help you avoid some of the common pitfalls of leading a group.

- *Losing sight of your objective.* Remember that your objective is to build spiritual multipliers, not just lead a Bible study group.

- *Lack of ministry with group members.* Your group will not begin to multiply spiritually unless you and your students develop a lifestyle of evangelism, follow-up, and discipleship. Much of this must take place outside the group meetings.

- *Lack of prayer.* Only the Holy Spirit can enable you and your students to multiply spiritually. A lack of prayer indicates a lack of dependence on God. Schedule time for prayer, so you will not put it off.

- *Weak selection of group members.* The temptation a leader faces is to allow people to be part of your group who are not faithful, available, and teachable. It is much better to

Step 5

train one person who goes on to train others than to have ten or fifteen people who never apply the principles.

- *Little personal involvement with members.* If you meet only during group time and an occasional ministry appointment, you will not be able to help them apply the principles of spiritual growth in their lifestyle. Plan social times too.

- *Leading a poor discussion time.* Leading a discussion is an art. As you become more experienced, you will find methods of discussion that fit your leadership style. Until then, remember these tips:

   Poor preparation can stifle discussion. Good preparation helps students get the greatest benefit from the lesson questions.

   Dominating leadership quenches discovery. Allowing everyone to share, ask questions, and express opinions or needs helps you better understand your group's strengths and weaknesses. It also makes members feel more valued.

   Asking ineffective questions, such as ones with yes and no answers, limits discussion. Good questions will help students think deeply and apply the principles to their lives.

   Little or no application will keep the discussion from becoming profitable. Pointing out the biblical principles and relating them to everyday life will help produce life changes.

- *Always doing everything the same way.* Every group has a tendency to fall into a routine. Spontaneity helps keep people alert and learning. Mix things up; add variety; and allow others to participate in different ways.

Action Point: Step 2 presented a chart called "Process for Building Multiplying Disciples." Refer to the chart as you prayerfully fill out each section of the following table. This table will help you plan your discipleship ministry in the weeks ahead.

Win	The people I have introduced to Christ are: The plans I have for witnessing in the next few weeks are:
Build	New Christian(s) I am following up are:
Train	New Christians or older Christians I can take with me witnessing are:
Send	Christians I believe would be interested in beginning a discipleship ministry are:
My Part	I feel God is leading me to participate in a discipleship ministry by:

Resources to Help You Make Disciples

Title	Unit Price	Qty.	Total
Five Steps Series			

Five Steps of Christian Growth
 This five-week study teaches new believers the biblical truth about salvation, steps to growing, understanding God's love, experiencing God's forgiveness, and being filled with the Holy Spirit.
    Leader's Guide
    Study Guide
	
	5.99
	3.99		

Five Steps to Sharing Your Faith
 This five-week study gives practical training on how to prepare a personal testimony, present the gospel clearly, guide new believers to assurance of salvation, and encourage fellowship in a good church.
    Leader's Guide
    Study Guide
	
	5.99
	3.99		

Transferable Concepts			
Transferable Concepts (Set of 10 books) Exciting tools to help you experience and share the abundant Christian life. Choose from individual books below:	19.50		
How You Can Be Sure You Are a Christian	1.99		
How You Can Experience God's Love and Forgiveness	1.99		
How You Can Be Filled With the Spirit	1.99		
How You Can Walk in the Spirit	1.99		
How You Can Be a Fruitful Witness	1.99		
How You Can Introduce Others to Christ	1.99		
How You Can Help Fulfill the Great Commission	1.99		
How You Can Love By Faith	1.99		

Title	Unit Price	Qty.	Total
How You Can Pray With Confidence	1.99		
How You Can Experience the Adventure of Giving	1.99		
Ten Basic Steps for Christian Maturity			
Ten Basic Steps A comprehensive curriculum for the Christian who wants to master the basics of Christian growth. Used by hundreds of thousands worldwide.			
The Ten Basic Steps Leader's Guide Contains Bible study outlines for teaching the complete series.	14.99		
A Handbook for Christian Maturity Combines the entire series of the *Ten Basic Steps* in one volume. A handy resource for private Bible study, an excellent book to help nurture spiritual growth and maturity.	16.99		
Introduction: The Uniqueness of Jesus	4.99		
Step 1: The Christian Adventure	4.99		
Step 2: The Christian and the Abundant Life	4.99		
Step 3: The Christian and the Holy Spirit	4.99		
Step 4: The Christian and Prayer	4.99		
Step 5: The Christian and the Bible	4.99		
Step 6: The Christian and Obedience	4.99		
Step 7: The Christian and Witnessing	4.99		
Step 8: The Christian and Giving	4.99		
Step 9: Exploring the Old Testament	4.99		
Step 10: Exploring the New Testament	4.99		

RESOURCES

Title	Unit Price	Qty.	Total
Other Resources Available			
A Man Without Equal (video) Intriguing 30-minute video explores the uniqueness of Jesus through dramatic re-creations and breathtaking portraits from the great Masters. An effective evangelism tool. This video can be used to help introduce others to Christ.	14.99		
A Man Without Equal (book) A fresh look at the unique birth, teachings, death, and resurrection of Jesus and how He continues to change the way we live and think. Good as an evangelistic tool.	4.99		
Four Spiritual Laws booklet (pkg. of 50) One of the most effective evangelistic tools ever developed. An easy-to-use way of sharing your faith with others.	8.99		
Spirit-Filled Life booklet (pkg. of 25) Discover the reality of the Spirit-filled life and how to live in moment-by-moment dependence on Him.	5.99		
Life Without Equal This book presents the length and breadth of the Christian's freedom in Jesus Christ and how believers can release Christ's resurrection power for life and ministry. Good for unbelievers or Christians who want to grow in their Christian life.	4.99		
Witnessing Without Fear A step-by-step guide to sharing your faith with confidence. Ideal for both individual and group study; a Gold Medallion winner.	9.99		

Reaching Your World Through Witnessing Without Fear
 This video package provides the resources you need to more effectively share the gospel with everyone in your world. Available in group and individual study versions.
     Group training package
     Individual study package
	
	69.95
	29.99		

"JESUS" Video This realistic, 120-minute video on the life of Christ will help you introduce your friends, neighbors, and loved ones to the life, death, and resurrection of Jesus.	25.99		

Title	Unit Price	Qty.	Total
The Holy Spirit: The Key to Supernatural Living This book helps you enter into the Spirit-filled life and shares how you can experience a life of supernatural power and victory.	7.99		
Keys to Dynamic Living (3×5 card; pkg. of 15) Experience a joyful, fruitful, Spirit-filled life and deal with temptation through "spiritual listening" and "spiritual breathing." Small enough to tuck into your pocket, purse, or Bible.	4.99		

BILLING INFORMATION

☐ Enclosed is my check payable to *NewLife Publications*

☐ Bill my MasterCard, VISA, or Discover card (circle one)

Card Number_____

Expiration Date_____ / _____

Signature_____

Subtotal all items _____

Less multiple purchase discount (see chart) _____

Add applicable sales tax for the following states: AL, CA, CO, CT, DC, FL, GA, IL, KS, KY, LA, MI, MN, MS, NC, NE, OH, RI, SC, VA, VT, WA, WI, WV, WY _____

Shipping & handling (see chart below) _____

Total Amount Due $ _____

DELIVERY ADDRESS

Name _____

Address _____

_____

City _____

State _____ Zip _____

Phone (_____) _____

SHIPPING AND HANDLING	
If Order Is	*Add*
< $10	$3.00
$10–$25	$3.50
$25–$50	$5.50
$50–$75	$7.50
> $75	$9.50

MAIL TO:

NewLife Publications
Campus Crusade for Christ
P.O. Box 593684
Orlando, FL 32859-3684
Phone orders: **800-235-7255**

MULTIPLE PURCHASE DISCOUNTS
5–9 items: 10% off • 10–19 items: 15% off
20–49 items: 20% off • 50+ items: 25% off

BILL BRIGHT is founder and president of Campus Crusade for Christ International. Serving in 155 major countries representing 98 percent of the world's population, he and his dedicated team of more than 113,000 full-time staff, associate staff, and trained volunteers have introduced tens of millions of people to Jesus Christ, discipling millions to live Spirit-filled, fruitful lives of purpose and power for the glory of God.

Dr. Bright did graduate study at Princeton and Fuller Theological seminaries from 1946 to 1951. The recipient of many national and international awards, including five honorary doctorates, he is the author of numerous books and publications committed to helping fulfill the Great Commission. His special focus is *NewLife2000*, an international effort to help reach more than six billion people with the gospel of our Lord Jesus Christ by the year 2000.

Response Form

☐ I have received Jesus Christ as my Savior and Lord as a result of reading this book.

☐ I am a new Christian and want to know Christ better and experience the abundant Christian life.

☐ I want to be one of the two million people who will join Dr. Bright in forty days of fasting and prayer for revival.

☐ Please send me **free** information on staff and ministry opportunities with Campus Crusade for Christ.

☐ Please send me **free** information about other books, booklets, audio cassettes, and videos by Bill Bright.

NAME_____

ADDRESS_____

CITY _____ STATE _____ ZIP _____

COUNTRY _____

Please check the appropriate box(es), clip, and mail this form in an envelope to:

      Dr. Bill Bright
      Campus Crusade for Christ
      P.O. Box 593684
      Orlando, FL 32859-3684

You may also fax your response to (407) 826-2149 or send E-mail to newlifepubs@ccci.org. Visit our Web site at www.newlifepubs.com.

This and other fine products from NewLife Publications are available from your favorite bookseller or by calling
(800) 235-7255, ext. 73 *(within U.S.) or*
(407) 826-2145, ext. 73 *(outside U.S.).*